HOMELESSNESS

Through the Eyes of a Nurse in the City

Crystal E. Barker

Poets Choice Publication
www.poetschoice.in
First Edition November 2022

Cover Design by Koni Deraz, Germany
Book Design by Adil Ilyas, Pakistan
Edited by
Wendy Burt-Thomas, Colorado, USA
Sandra Dsouza, India
Reviewed by Angela Barker Thomas, Kentucky, USA

ISBN: 978-93-95193-27-6
BCID: 706-16712951
www.bookcrossing.com
Price: $25

ACKNOWLEDGEMENTS/ABOUT THIS COLLECTION

——

All of these poems are the original work of this submitting author.

None of these poems have been previously published or are in consideration by any other locations/entities.

Of note, this collection is written in the poetic form of the Pleiades—seven lines for the constellation of seven sisters and six syllables on each line representing the nearly invisible nature of one sister. Forty nine poems were written—symbolism of the seven lines of each poem and the seven sisters (7x7 = 49). As with this form, there are one word titles, and the first letter of each line is to begin with the first letter of the title. For the symbolism and power of the topic of HOMELESSNESS, each poem began with the letter H.

This book is dedicated to those who have felt the cold of the street, who have read the pages of an eviction, who have heard the words of their loved one casting them out, who have smelled the sour from lack of hygiene, or who have craved the taste of a home with a spirit of love and acceptance.

TESTIMONIALS

---

1. Crystal Barker has made a home in the hearts of every reader for each person featured in her most recent book, Homelessness Through The Eyes Of A Nurse In The City. She has restored their sense of belonging while reminding us of the common thread that unites us as humans- suffering; and the need now, more than ever, to show kindness and compassion to all.
    Michelle Zeller
    Clinical Neuropsychologist, Friend, and Colleague
    Los Angeles, California, USA

2. Each of these tiny poems is a sundog amid storm clouds.... an acknowledgement of human survival. Life's ironies and grace are condensed then magnified thru the compassionate prism of Crystal's pen. After reading this book, home has never seemed so dear.
    Angela Barker Thomas
    Sister, Poet, and Fan
    Kentucky, USA

3. As I read these poems, I experienced a walk through the lives of the homeless. Their struggles were revealed in a raw and compassionate way. I am humbled by each uniquely written line.
    Laura Ruth Hogston
    Poet and Chaplain, Pastoral Counselor Addiction Recovery Care
    Kentucky, USA

4. In this collection of Crystal Barker's poetry, we, the readers, are forced to taste, touch, and smell the realities of humans who live without shelter. Restricted by the Pleiades form, the poet magically manipulates words, with passion, wisdom and powerful imagery. Crystal has a story to tell. I, for one, shall not be able to look away.

    Juanita Mays
    Author, Poet
    Ohio, USA

5. Crystal Barker has a beautiful way of expressing people's deepest concerns and feelings in her poetry. In this book, Homelessness Through The Eyes Of A Nurse In The City, she so keenly and accurately describes what it is like to be homeless and also what it is like to feel the pain of seeing a homeless human being suffering. She inspires through her poetry the active role we each can play in bettering the world for our fellow human beings. Her poems are real and heart warming, and always a joy to read.

    Mojgan Saber
    MD, Colleague, Friend
    Los Angeles, California, USA

TABLE OF CONTENTS

01 - HOBO...8

02 - HIDDEN..9

03 - HATES...10

04 - HANDPICKING..11

05 - HOPE...12

06 - HAZY...13

07 - HUNTER...14

08 - HISTORY..15

09 - HOLEY..16

10 - HEALTH..17

11 - HEISTS..18

12 - HOUR..19

13 - HUCKS..20

14 - HELLO...21

15 - HURRAY...22

16 - HIERARCHY...23

17 - HERONS'..24

18 - HOLLERS..25

19 - HOMEWORK...26

20 - HOLIDAY..27

21 - HEARS...28

22 - HYMNS...29

23 - HUES...30

24 - HEIGHTENED..31

25 - HONORED..32

26 - HIPS..33

27 - HUGE...34

28 - HEELS..35

29 - HARDLY..36

30 - HEARSE...37

31 - HALLUCINATIONS 38

32 - HOLY...39

33 - HOOD..40

34 - HUMVEE..41

35 - HOP...42

36 - HINT..43

37 - HOTBEDS...44

38 - HUNGER...45

39 - HOLDS..46

40 - HEARLDING..47

41 - HURLED..48

42 - HEALTHCARE..49

43 - HURT...50

44 - HANDCRAFTED 51

45 - HIBERNATES...52

46 - HAWK..53

47 - HEDGE..54

48 - HALLELUJAH..55

49 - HEART..56

01

HOBO

Hillbilly girl leaves home,

hustles to *big city*.

Has never seen unhoused.

Halves her Big Mac with him.

Hobo smiles with surprise!

Have shared conversation.

Here, they sit *as equals*.

02

HIDDEN

Here, on the cold hard street,

he pulls mangled blanket

high above shoulders bare.

He is camouflaged now,

hidden behind park bench.

He sleeps, invisible;

head filled with dreams of *Home*.

03

HATES

———

He, the law enforcer

hates this part of the job!

Has to tell her, move on.

How does he do this task?

Have few options to give;

he converses with her.

He hands her his packed lunch.

04

HANDPICKING

—

Harvesters flood the fields.

Huts of cardboard for night. . . .

Handpicking during day

hanging fruits, veggies, nuts.

Half of America

has eaten from their hands.

Head home—when season done.

05

HOPE

——

Had once, house, wife and kids.

Hard liquor became vice,

his favorite—vodka.

Heineken, Bud and Coors

he would take if no choice.

Hence, lost license—car—job.

Hangs hope now on twelve steps!

HAZY

———

He still loves to watch sports;

hangs out in the alley,

happy the bar owner,

hosting the *Laker's* fans,

hoists lowered window shades.

Here, he watches the game,

hazy window view free.

07

HUNTER

Hunter and gatherer;

his instincts come alive!

Hunts cans for an income. . . .

Hungry for fine dinner,

he fishes amongst reeds.

Hot skillet on fire pit

hisses with fresh fillet.

HISTORY

Husbanded, a good wife,

handled like a *punchbag*.

How many more bruises?

Hastily, she has fled.

Her mind was determined

history not to repeat.

Her savior now, a pimp. . . .

09

HOLEY

———

Hollow are his blue eyes.

Holey oversized pants.

Has little faith—life will

hail better tomorrow.

Has bench to claim tonight.

Housed like a turtle's shell

hard plastic shields from fog.

10

HEALTH

Hunched over on bus bench,

has no place to lie flat.

Her edematous legs—

heavy with extra fluid.

Heart failure soon follows!

Health not good on the street;

hourglass marks her time.

11

HEISTS

He's aware, *illegal.*

Has to remain mobile.

Heists shopping cart at night.

Holds precious possessions.

His most dear, warm blanket.

He pulls up to trash can,

hoists half donut for meal!

12

HOUR

Hour hand dark strikes midnight.

Her community roused,

horns and sirens screaming!

Hypnotizing flames flit.

Households reduced to ash. . . .

Hundreds have lost their homes.

Horror watched on TV.

13

HUCKS

—

His depression freezes

him to paralysis.

Had time to relocate.

health department weighs in—

heavy equipment comes;

hucks tent into dumpster.

Hedge flattened—but not hope.

14

HELLO

———

He is released today...

has served ten years in pen.

Has no transportation;

housing is unsecured.

Hard labor he knows not.

Has no job, where to turn?

Hello world, he is free!

15

HURRAY

—

Hurray, it's his birthday!

His foster mother sings.

Has chocolate frosted cake.

He is an adult now.

Heaves large pack on his back,

his decision to go.

Husky arms wave *goodbye*.

16

HIERARCHY

Highway crosses river.

Hidden under the bridge,

habitat—*underworld.*

Hierarchy determines

how prime space divided.

Having been newest here,

his niche, is on damp dirt.

17

HERONS'

Herded out of city,

hillside becomes his place.

Haven was meant to be

herons' sanctuary.

Holstered onto the trees,

hammers tent line anchors.

Howls at moon, through treetops.

18

HOLLERS

Hears voices in his mind,

head spinning like record.

He whispers back to them,

hiding lips inside cup.

He's suspicious of all.

Hunkers in corner seat.

Hollers out, "Go away!"

19

HOMEWORK

He lives with mom in car.

Homework is hard to do;

honking horns passing by.

His papers are wrinkled.

He shows up faithfully;

Hopes—no one can smell him.

Happy though, got an A!

20

HOLIDAY

___

Holiday coming soon.

Hazy are memories:

hears clatter in kitchen,

handles hot on stovetop,

ham's sweet smell wafts on air.

His taste buds— now craving

homemade pies of *Mother's*.

21

HEARS

—

Hair matted, enters train.

Harsh odor permeates,

heavy pants— soiled with stains;

hem fell out long ago.

Here, he is at least warm.

Hears clacking wheels on track.

He will sleep to white noise.

22

HYMNS

—

His job downsized, abrupt;

had no unemployment.

His church—important still,

hewed spot in nearby weeds.

Hymns beckon through the door.

His faith—unshakable,

he kneels, prays for others!

23

HUES

Hidden in our plain sight,

harbor across front yard.

Housed yachts worth a million.

Houses there even more.

Here they will make their camp,

hues of earth colored tarps;

hope to stay, transparent.

24

HEIGHTENED

Housing crisis looms large.

How to fit anymore?

Heavy cranes work magic.

Hints of tower Babel.

High rises fill skyline,

heightened and multiplied.

HUD vouchers, for a few.

25

HONORED

—

Honored, cat trails along.

He awaits soft caress. . . .

High, waves black, fluffy tail.

He is not bothered by

his master's homelessness.

He learned some lives ago,

home is where the heart is.

26

HIPS

Half of buttocks exposed.

Hips narrowed by hunger,

hanging pants like scarecrow.

Holds cup for donation;

hardly matters why here.

Have you spare change Madam?

Have mercy, have mercy!

27

HUGE

——

He stops at the crossroads

his car worth 80 grand.

Huge encampment on right,

he nervously takes peek.

His light soon signals Go.

His mind gives no more thought,

has belief—never him.

28

HEELS

—

Hiking is not joyful.

Heels black from exposure,

heat travels through his shoes.

Hot pavement burns his soles.

Has foot rot as result.

Hazard now, infection.

Hygiene is hard to do!

29

HARDLY

—

How does he defecate

having no privacy?

His arthritic joints ache;

hardly can squat in place.

Hears no one, sighs relief!

Hides buttocks against wall.

Hurries away from mess.

30

HEARSE

—

Hears wife's diagnosis.

Hope for 10% chance,

house mortgaged for a cure.

Hundreds thousands later,

hearse carries her away.

He sleeps now, cold outside.

Heaven and *she* above. . . .

31

HALLUCINATIONS

Heroin is her friend,

holds her hand when lonely;

hides her fear from the world.

Hallucinations feed

hungry soul that's empty.

Her mother prays for her,

has funeral pre-paid.

32

HOLY

Hallowed is not his name!

How dare he breach such trust?

Holy man of the cloth

has ruined innocence.

Having lasting effects,

his lost boys, walk street now;

hiding from guilt and shame.

33

HOOD

———

Here he straps US flag.

Hooks sheets over windows.

His truck—now his castle.

Hardship better endured

having a companion.

Hood ornament canine

holds vigil—like a knight.

34

HUMVEE

His commander in chief

hosts a White House dinner;

handshakes with movie stars.

Halfway around the world,

Humvee locked and loaded,

he has no home today.

Hump it Marine, OORAH!

35

HOP

———

Have homeless on your streets?

How do you clean your town?

Hand them one way ticket

hoping they go away.

"Hop on that Greyhound now,

head West to land of dreams!"

Here they come—Hollywood.

36

HINT

How she sits on the chair,

high chin, upright, regal.

Hands still soft like butter.

Her clothes not yet crumpled.

Hint of eyeshadow still.

Hope reflects from wide eyes.

Has not been homeless, long.

37

HOTBEDS

Haves battle the *Have Nots.*

Hope to clean neighborhood.

Hell's fury is unleashed,

hails fire onto their tents!

High swirling flames play tag.

Hotbeds go up in smoke.

Have to move along now.

38

HUNGER

How ironic he thinks,

holding up a new sign.

Had passed this way before. . . .

Hardly noticed who stood

hours on end in road.

Here, now he is begging,

hunger forces lost pride.

39

HOLDS

Her youth has been taken.

Hair raising screams escape

her trembling red lips.

Husband of her mother,

having had her, his way—

holds open door to street.

Her story and She, gone. . . .

10

HEARLDING

———

Her stage, Metro station.

Her fingers love to dance,

hopping along the strings.

Heirloom violin sings,

heralding tunes aloft.

Harried businessmen pause;

heart's beats—calmed at day's end.

41

HURLED

Hurled painfully away,

his father yells, "Leave now.

Homo son of mine will

have no place in this home.

Hell-bound you are for sure. . . .

Heaven is only for

heterosexuals!"

42

HEALTHCARE

___

He scales high border wall,

haloed vision in mind.

Here in America,

healthcare, education.

Hands of a skilled mason

hardened with years long toil.

Have room for another?

43

HURT

—

Homeless camp cooking pit,

heralded as cause of

horrifying wildfire!

Hot flames escaped their grasp.

Homes burned and acres scorched.

Hurt firemen paid a price.

Hunger's clutch, affects all.

44

HANDCRAFTED

———

High above the river

hanging off bridge trestle

heavy beams hold pallets.

Hand crafted living space.

Heights achieved by ladders

hoarded from dumpsters near.

Home sweet home for this week.

45

HIBERNATES

———

His spot under the bush

hugs popular bike path.

Here he went to sleep, tired!

Heat beats down from the sun.

Hibernates on blanket.

His vulnerable state

harks passing onlookers.

46

HAWK

—

High above the city

his empire reigns over

homeless camp, encroaching

hallowed space of business.

How will he disperse them?

Hawk thinks same about him,

Hanging on metal ledge. . . .

47

HEDGE

He always loved his books.

Hedges of library

hides him for the moment.

His belly growls for bread.

His mind so craves stories.

Has no money for lunch.

He feasts, on books instead.

48

HALLELUJAH

He resides in a tent.

Hungers for beauty—still.

He tills soil in the front;

his garden thrives with love.

He plants cross at doorway.

Has more than some—he says.

Hallelujah, a home!

19

HEART

———

Huge, it's overwhelming.

Hurts to think about it.

Heart so desires to help!

How does one even start?

Here's a sandwich sister.

Here's a notebook, young child.

Here's socks and boots, brother.

CPSIA information can be obtained
at www.ICGtesting.com
Printed in the USA
BVHW012040210223
658927BV00012B/276

9 789395 193276